Software Engineering today

Guiding principles for creating a quicker and better software

Epris E. Ezekiel

Contents

Introduction 1

Chapter 1: How Common Software Engineering Is 3

Chapter 2: How to be a successful software engineer 13

Chapter 3: Other steps to becoming a successful software Engineer 20

Chapter 4: How other fields connect to software engineering 30

Conclusion.. 38

Introduction

Software engineers are responsible for creating and designing computer programs and applications. Software engineers have a variety of employment options to select from given their strong demand across many industries.

History of software Engineering

When Margaret Hamilton was developing the software for the Apollo spacecraft in 1963, she coined the phrase "software engineering." Software development is currently in a bind as it tries to stay up with the developments in hardware development. At this time, new programs and languages were introduced, which helped to advance software engineering.

The much-needed boost for the software engineering industry came from the NATO Software Engineering Conference, which took place in 1968 and 1969.

Software engineering had become a recognized discipline alongside computer science and traditional engineering by the 1980s.

Chapter 1: How Common Software Engineering Is

The following are important elements that support the widespread acceptance of software engineering:

• Big Software: In real life, building a wall as opposed to a house or other construction is considerably more comfortable. Similar to how software increases in size, software engineering assists in its development.

• Scalability: If the software development process was based on scientific and technical principles, it would be simpler to create new software from scratch in order to scale an existing one.

• **Adaptability:** Creating new software using software engineering was simple when the development of software was based on engineering and science.

- **Cost:** The hardware industry has proven its mettle, and extensive production has lowered the cost of computers and other technology.

- **Dynamic nature:** The program is always growing and changing. This depends on the user's working environment. Software development can be done more effectively by using quality management to create high-quality software products.

How to Begin as a Software Engineer

Up until recently, the only way to properly start a career as a software engineer was to have a two- or four-year degree in computer science.

Other math and science-related degrees in fields like information systems, electronics, and civil engineering, as well as community college courses, have also helped people get into the software development profession.

But, a formal degree or a few college courses are no longer the only means to become a web developer.

Coding boot camps are becoming more and more popular as a quick route to a career in software engineering.

Coding boot camps are intense, eight- to thirty-week programs that place an emphasis on developing programming skills in particular languages while typically addressing the fundamentals of information technology.

In order to get students ready to enter the IT job market as soon as possible, most boot camps focus on the skills that are in great demand online or in a specific area.

Before choosing a curriculum, consider the type of employment you want and the languages you should master.

What Exactly Do Software Engineers Do?

Operating systems and applications for computers are created by computer software developers. They work with system programmers, analysts, and other engineers to design systems, project capabilities, and select performance interfaces.

User needs analysis, design element guidance, and software installation management are additional services provided by software engineers for computers. While building software systems to project results, engineers must take into account mathematical models and scientific analysis.

Software engineers continue to be in high demand. The Bureau of Labor Statistics projects that employment of software developers, analysts, and testers will increase by 25% between 2021 and 2031, five times faster than the national average (BLS).

Since most organizations use software, professionals in computer software can work in almost any industry. The BLS predicts that there will be 682,000 additional jobs in computer and information technology.

As businesses' software requirements get more complex, they need software engineers to create new programming tools and applications.

An application is built, developed, and tested by a software engineer to ensure that it satisfies user demands after considering those needs. Software engineers have a lot to do. A competent software developer need to be able to:

- Create systems together while gathering data on their potential, performance requirements, and interactions with other professionals such as engineers, programmers, and systems analysts.
- Resolve bugs in current software, simplify its compatibility with new technologies, and boost overall performance.
- To determine a design's viability given the time and financial constraints, analyze user needs and software specs.
- Have customer meetings to go over software system development and upkeep.
- Arrange for the installation of the software system and keep an eye on the essential hardware to ensure it is functioning properly.

- As you create, develop, and modify software systems, incorporate mathematical models and scientific analysis to assess the effects of those designs.

- Develop and oversee testing, validation, programming, and documentation procedures for software systems.

- Information analysis can be used to determine, advise, and arrange computer specs, layouts, and adjustments to peripheral equipment.

- Lead technical, technological, and programming teams in addition to other engineers and scientists.

- Before deciding on the hardware configuration, get and assess the necessary reporting formats, associated costs, and security requirements.

- Set performance criteria for the system.

- Instruction in using new or modernized equipment.

- Data must be saved, retrieved, and updated in order to assess system requirements and capabilities.
- Provide suggestions for environmental control devices for system installation, such as dust suppression, temperature regulation, and humidity levels.

The Essential soft Skills for Software Engineers

- **Communication:** Teamwork, problem-solving, and communication skills are essential for software engineers. They may organize with other team members to collaborate on the same project, explain a product to a customer, or update their management on their progress.

- **Multitasking:** Software engineers may need to swiftly move between projects or divide their attention between different modules of the same project when working on a deadline or attending to the needs of the team.

- **Organization:** To oversee numerous projects through their various stages and keep track of details, software engineers must demonstrate a certain level of organization. While overseeing large teams, busy managers must act fast to gather information at a client's request.

- **Detail-Orientation:** Software engineers need to be extremely attentive. As it would seem, they have a variety of ongoing projects to keep track of, troubleshoot, and retain extensive information about.

Core hard skills for software engineers

- **Data Structures:** Data structures and algorithms are tools used by programmers and software engineers to build computer applications. Engineers' familiarity with data structures and algorithms helps them create efficient and well-optimized code.

- **Software testing:** To evaluate and confirm features and functionality, software developers test new programs and applications. This improves performance and fixes errors. They also need to be familiar with the software development process in order to plan, test, and deploy systems.

- **Programming Languages:** Software engineers use programming languages to write the code for computer programs and applications. Among the popular languages are Python, C++, and Java.

- **Understanding of core computer concepts:** Software engineers need to be well-versed in concepts like databases, operating systems, and computer networking. A range of operating systems, including Linux, and database management systems like SQL, must be understood by professionals.

Chapter 2: How to be a successful software engineer

Being a superb software engineer and writing programs are quite different things. Consider yourself a software engineer, and programming and coding are only a result of that. Almost anyone can become adept enough in a language's syntax and layout with a little practice to start building programs.

So what qualities do successful software engineers have? Beyond developing codes and programs, how do you advance? It goes without saying that it's essential to understand and grasp the foundations. While there are numerous platforms and resources available for studying the principles of programming, possessing a broad variety of supporting skills is also necessary in order to become a good software engineer.

These skills are much more difficult to perfect and require ongoing work and practice. Some subjects are unsuitable for course study. Yet there are some programming-related behaviors and routines you may get into that will help you develop the necessary skills over time and become a better software engineer.

You must take the following actions:

1. **Select a suitable language:**

There are numerous distinct programming languages available. So the key is to advance slowly. It's not easy to pick a reliable programming language that fits your project well and advances your goals. Hence, finish each work before going on.

It is essential to choose the correct language because it tells a computer to follow the instructions regularly, which will help you avoid having to perform the same tasks repeatedly. Instead, the application might finish it automatically for you.

The greatest solutions are those that are straightforward to extend, debug, fix, and document when you choose a language that suits the objectives of your project. Yet, we may claim that choosing an ideal and fruitful programming language is the secret to success.

2. Keep your language positive

As we all know, there is always something new, and if things are not going your way, you could feel like giving up. Take a break in these times, then come back stronger. One thing to always keep in mind is that since there is a solution for everything, specialists and developers never lose up.

3. Identify modest goals

Avoid attempting to use every programming language. Make sure to specify modest goals before moving on to complex and important ones. If you want to do well, make sure to give each task your full attention and focus. This is the best tactic for increasing confidence. Always strive to develop your abilities and produce more.

4. Consider your soft skills

While having a broad knowledge of programming languages is wonderful, you also need to be an expert in soft skills if you want to quickly advance to the top

5%. Soft skills are essential for software developers since they allow for fruitful social engagement.

Developing your problem-solving, communication, self-learning, time management, adaptability, responsibility, teamwork, and cooperation skills can make you more competitive.

5. Push yourself instead of others

You should first compete with yourself before competing with others. Never compare yourself to other people; instead, focus on improving yourself and monitoring your development over time. You'll lose motivation and face a lot of challenges if you compare yourself to other people.

6. Keep a "never-give-up" attitude

The path to success is not easy, and there are many challenges along the way. If you want to be successful in accomplishing your goals, you must invest a lot of time and energy into your trip. Yet things might not always work in your favor. Being a successful programmer requires a variety of skills, one of which is having a never-say-die attitude.

You'll be astonished at how quickly you catch up on new concepts and start putting them into practice once you get used to it. Just remember that beginning something new is never simple.

7. Use the best development tools

When creating software, be sure to choose the tools that are best for the job. for instance, your IDE. Use the same caution while selecting your IDE as you would when selecting hardware. As said, choose an editor and become an authority in it. By using top-notch tools, you can reduce the length of time spent developing by half. You invest a lot of money, but you also wind up saving time.

8. Refer to online guides and tutorials

Today, one of the finest ways to learn new things, practice exercises, and take formative assessments is to watch online tutorials. It is an excellent way for a beginner to start their growth journey. More swiftly than ever before, you can learn new skills and technologies.

9. Put in a lot of effort

No one will ever give you a wage increase or a promotion without payment. While it is considered that hard work pays off, putting in the time is not enough; you also need to be useful and productive.

10. Always ask for help when you need it

This is one of the quickest ways to overcome challenges and move forward. Don't second-guess yourself when you need help; just ask for it. Never be reluctant to approach your friends and mentors for help if you need it while you are studying. Even if your questions seem apparent or absurd, don't be afraid to ask.

11. Consistency outweighs intensity

It is better to read about your field for at least 40 minutes each day to satisfy heavy studying workloads than to sit in front of a computer all day.

Don't you believe you must have studied this in college? Stress levels were easier to manage when homework was completed in smaller chunks during the school day rather than all at once.

Chapter 3: Other steps to becoming a successful software Engineer

- **Create an architecture for each software package**

Never begin coding an application without first developing a solid architecture plan. Design patterns, SOLID principles, domain-driven design, and other methods are helpful. Before building the program, architecture should be focused on to save time later and lessen the prevalence of spaghetti codes, which makes software engineering difficult.

With each new application or piece of software you create, your application architecture skills must improve. You'll be more productive and end up with code that is cleaner if you separate the coding and architecture portions of the process. If you can learn how to separate your repository and service layer from the application, you can develop things much more quickly. You'll also be competent at handling challenging testing.

As you learn more about the MVC paradigm, the importance and obviousness of software design will become more apparent. Many software engineers find it challenging to construct large-scale corporate systems; nevertheless, knowing how to design an architecture before starting to write will help you see things clearly.

- **Develop Strict Test Cases**

Another crucial skill you must develop if you want to grow in the field of software engineering is writing test cases for your application. When writing your unit tests, test-driven development (TDD) is vital.

Prior to writing implementations, test cases should direct function design and output prediction, according to the TDD technique. Beginners might find it challenging, but software engineers will benefit greatly from using this approach once they get started. By employing a TDD technique, you may write cleaner code to ensure that the apps you create are always manageable.

At this point, it's critical to keep in mind that you might not be able to create tests for every scenario. You must therefore get the talent of knowing which scenarios may and cannot be tested. As an illustration, imagine creating a function called Add(+) to add two variables. For this, a TDD technique and a variety of test cases can easily be generated. But, if your software displays the data in ViewModel, you might not need to create test cases for it.

In general, creating tests often can help you redesign your software application and architecture more successfully. Additionally, it will enable you to provide features with few to no delays.

- **Create blogs and articles to chronicle your learnings**

Keeping a record of your ideas and learnings may be quite beneficial for your long-term skill development. Your software engineering learnings can be documented in a diary, blog, or website. You'll be more likely to remember concepts you've just learned if you write articles about them. You'll also learn newer nuances you might have missed.

According to studies, the more you write down information, the easier it will be for you to remember and comprehend. Also, you open the door to opinions from other programmers all around the world by compiling your lessons learnt and publicizing them in a blog or on social media. You have two options: either you can heed their advice and improve what you do, or you can correct them if they're wrong.

In any event, you will have established a line of communication, which will be very beneficial to you as a software developer. You may have noticed that most software engineers working for top IT companies routinely post blogs where they discuss their skills and experiences. You should try to get a similar result!

- **Acquaint yourself with version control systems**

Being knowledgeable about version control systems will help you become a better software developer.

Regardless matter whether you use GitHub or another version control platform, the objective should be to thoroughly educate yourself in version control and code management. You'll use version control systems frequently as a software engineer, either to download your teammates' work or to commit and update your own.

Software engineers are allowed to work remotely thanks to version control technologies. Once you're at ease with version control systems, you'll be able to manage your code changes and collaborate with any developer from any place.

- **Make use of Kanban Boards**

Make it a habit to have a Kanban board where you may post all of your issues, bugs, ideas, to-dos, etc. Using this program, you may quickly view items such as Progress Items, To-Do List, Finished Items, Problems Arising, and more. You can also create your own boards based on the methodology you want.

You will therefore benefit from becoming familiar with how these tools work and how to use them for increased productivity. As a software engineer, you can use Kanban boards for so many things, like taking notes, organizing tasks, and creating to-do lists.

The main focus of software engineering is problem solving. Investigate several approaches to problem-solving When you're not addressing coding errors for clients, you'll be helping your colleagues. One of the most important difficulties that software developers tackle is the optimization of the algorithms used to run software.

Hence, as you develop your software engineering talents, make sure to consider all potential solutions. You might try utilizing lists if an issue can be fixed using the array data structure to see if the code gets better or worse. You can think creatively and find new ways to address problems by integrating and comparing numerous ideas.

As a general rule, always assess the speed of the algorithms that are utilized to generate the code. Maintain consistency while contrasting the temporal complexity of alternative strategies by using Big O notation. ,, a, in the ofa,s of thea, in thea, in the, in the, a, vs. Moreover, it will let you produce excellent outcomes with few to no bugs.

How to create top-notch software

- **Create or collaborate with a stellar team:**

Whether you're working on a project internally or with a third party, put the correct team in place. Of course, this team needs to have the requisite programming and coding skills, but the best teams go above and beyond.

Teams who are able to work together to create amazing things have found a method to reconcile their love of coding and their need to be profitable. These teams can maintain a project and meet deadlines. Although it may seem like a simple process, everyone who has ever worked on a large project understands how easy it is to stray from the intended direction.

- **Gather facts while maintaining objectivity:**

Will your seemingly amazing concept actually succeed, even if you think it will? Do user and market research. Distribute questionnaires to potential users. Ask questions. Analyze your information. Right now, focus more on the idea's potential as a whole and less on the intricacies of the interface. Even if you may be passionate about your project, others might not be. Be impartial and receptive to recommendations.

- **Have a defined goal:**

You may avoid showing up at the bottom of the app store search results by concentrating on a certain feature set for your app. Make a list of your KPIs right away to aid in prioritizing later. The number of users or downloads may be one of such KPIs, but you may also have additional metrics.

- **Have a plan:**

If you have a goal, how will you achieve it? Your team must create a strategy for each component of the app or program from start to finish.

- **Maintain focus:**

"What if the app did this, too?" Scope creep is a fairly prevalent issue. Think about whether that innovative idea is necessary for this launch. If it improves and increases the marketability of the program is one thing.

If it's "nice to have," you can add it later. It might also merit its own application if it is deserving. As time is money, losing track actually costs money. The longer it takes for your app to get traction and begin generating revenue, the more features you should include right immediately.

- **Be flexible:**

While staying on plan is crucial, your exceptional team must be ready to alter course or make adjustments as necessary. One of the many reasons we like the Agile way of software development is because it gives you the freedom to add or adjust as needed every two weeks.

- **Communicate:**

The most important—and frequently disregarded—factor is communication. Teams cannot succeed without it. The final result is not what you had in mind, deadlines are missed, and people make mistakes. As we said at the outset, choose a team that can communicate well. So be sure to make everything obvious to them as well. You want to make sure that your concept and your objectives are understood and communicated throughout the entire process.

Chapter 4: How other fields connect to software engineering

- **Computer programming Languages**

Software engineering's influence on programming languages is evident. Programming languages are the primary instruments used in the production of software. As a result, they had a big influence on our capacity to complete our software engineering tasks.

The development of programming languages is then impacted by these advancements. Perhaps the most well-known example of this impact is supported by the ability of modern programming languages to promote collaborative development of huge projects by allowing modularity characteristics like separate and autonomous compilation and the separation of concept from implementation.

The ADA programming language, for instance, makes it easier to construct packages by enabling the separation of the packages' interface from their implementation, and it contains a library of packages that may be used as components in the development of independent software systems.

This is a step toward enabling software to be created piece by piece from a catalog of easily available components, similar to how hardware is put together. The development of object-oriented programming languages like C++ is a key step for rapid software development.

- **Operating Systems**

Because operating systems were the first truly enormous software systems to be created, software engineering was necessary for their creation. This has caused operating systems to have a significant impact on software engineering. Many of the earliest ideas for software design came from early attempts to construct operating systems.

Two examples of how software engineering techniques have influenced operating system architectures are operating systems that are built with a small secured kernel that provided the bare minimum of functionality for interacting with the peripherals and a non-protected component that provided the majority of the functionality formerly associated with operating systems. For instance, the user may be able to manipulate the paging strategy, which is typically regarded as an essential element of the operating system, through the non-protected area.

The command language interpreter played a significant role in the development of early operating systems. It is currently viewed as just another piece of utility software. For instance, it is now possible for every user to have a different interpreter thanks to this. On UNIX platforms, there are normally at least three different types.

- **Database**

Databases are a different class of significant software systems that have been created and have influenced software engineering by introducing new design techniques. The concept of data-indigence, another illustration of the separation of specification and implementation, is maybe the database industry's greatest contribution to software engineering.

The database allows for the creation of applications employing user data without having to worry about how the data is actually represented.

Another noteworthy impact that database technology has had on software engineering is the capability to integrate database systems as components of large-scale software systems.

Databases have previously addressed the multiple problems connected to the regulation of concurrent access to enormous volumes of information by numerous users, therefore there is no need to reinvent these answers when creating software systems. Instead, we can incorporate a component from an existing database system.

- **Artificial intelligence**

Artificial intelligence is a different field that has had an impact on software engineering. Techniques that are backed by artificial intelligence apply logic in both the specifications for software and the syntax of programming languages.

The logic orientation seems to be bridging the gap between specification and implementation by raising the level of implementation language higher than before. The logic-based approach to specification and programming is sometimes referred to as declarative. The objective is to define needs rather than procedurally describe them; this results in an executable declarative description. The use of logic programming languages like PROLOG makes this strategy simpler.

Software engineering methods are used by artificial intelligence systems that are more current. The fact that these systems are modularized makes it easy to distinguish between the rules that the expert systems use to process the data, such as a rule to determine a course of action, and the facts that the expert systems are aware of.

Specializations in software engineering as a career

A degree in software engineering and relevant experience are prerequisites for many computing jobs. Software engineers can pursue well-paying jobs and career advancement, albeit the specific opportunities will vary depending on their degree, sector, and location.

- **Developer:** A full-stack developer is one that works on both front-end and back-end programming. These professionals are adept at a number of programming languages. They design and develop full websites and applications, including the structural and graphical elements.

- **Information security analyst:** Information security analysts closely monitor their companies' computer networks in order to spot, stop, and investigate security problems. They regularly take care of software maintenance and updates, look for security gaps in firewalls and data encryption, and take the necessary safeguards to safeguard sensitive information.

- **Programmer:** A professional coder tasked with writing, modifying, and testing the scripts that power software applications and programs is known as a computer programmer. Programmers and software developers work closely together to convert designs into the code that a computer needs to run. The job necessitates familiarity with several programming languages.

- **Data Scientist:** A data scientist gathers and examines structured and unstructured data in order to identify market trends, business needs, and other patterns. A data scientist typically holds a degree in computer engineering or data science in addition to a background in math, statistics, or economics.

- **Systems Analyst:** A systems analyst is a computer expert who maintains and keeps track of an organization's IT systems. They collaborate with many departments to address technological difficulties in order to ensure that business requirements are consistent with the company's technologies.

Conclusion

The greatest way to learn new things is to pick something you're interested in; anything that feels more like a duty or a task than a source of pleasure and fulfillment will not stick with you. Look for strategies to improve learning enjoyment. Learning should be joyful.

Never, ever be afraid of failing! The more attempts we make at something, the more likely it is that we will succeed. Failure only happens when you give up trying to improve. So go ahead and start learning!

I sincerely hope this article will help you develop into a better software engineer who is fantastic at creating better software.